TAT WALE BABA

RISHI
OF THE
HIMALAYAS

by
Vincent J. Daczynski

YOGI
VINCE
BOOKS

Published 2022
by
YogiVinceBooks LLC

ISBN: 978-0-578-38093-3

Other Books by the Author:
For Sales' Sake Meditate!
It's About Time!

Cover photograph: Tat Wale Baba

Table of Contents

Preface

God is the same everywhere.
It is men who make him different.
~ Tat Wale Baba

Tat Wale Baba. Photograph by Vincent J. Daczynski

According to Vedic scripture, the mere sight of a yogi saint is sufficient to transform an individual's life from the pursuit of mundane pleasures to the pursuit of wisdom and God realization. My personal experience bears truth to this statement. I was profoundly influenced by the sight of Sri Tat Wale Baba, and my brief two hours' encounter with him. Sri Tat Wale Baba was the living

1

embodiment of the Vedas. He did not have to speak or preach. He exhibited those qualities about which other yogis only preach. His presence radiated a divine essence that, of itself, communicated the goal of life to all who had the honor to come within his aura.

This book was written out of my deep admiration and respect for Sri Tat Wale Baba. It is a tribute to one of the world's greatest twentieth-century yogis who, because of his reclusive lifestyle, has received little publicity outside of India. It is the intent of this book to memorialize Sri Tat Wale Baba for the many people who knew and loved him. Of further intent is to introduce the Western world and all seekers of God to Sri Tat Wale Baba so that they might glimpse (albeit in book format) the life of an enlightened yogi.

Introduction

In December 1988 I returned to India to retrace a path I traveled about twenty years earlier when I made a pilgrimage to Rishikesh to pursue spiritual unfoldment. I was trying to relive that short time in my life when I was blessed to find secret India.

In the spring of 1969 I had been extremely fortunate to attend a training course with a god-realized saint, His Holiness Maharishi Mahesh Yogi. It was one of the greatest experiences of my life. During that time, I was also fortunate to meet Sri Tat Wale Baba when he came to lecture to our group at Maharishi's academy.

Tat Wale Baba with Maharishi Mahesh Yogi to his right.
Photograph by Vincent J. Daczynski.

Since then, however, Tat Wale Baba had entered mahasamadhi and Maharishi had moved his ashram to the peaceful and secluded farm fields of Noida. Therefore, it was not possible for me to experience the past. Nevertheless, my return to India gave me the impetus to document the life of Sri Tat Wale Baba, one of India's greatest yogis.

CHAPTER 1

The Early Years

Laxman Jhula Bridge gives pilgrims easy access to the many ashrams along the Ganges.
Photograph by Vincent J. Daczynski.

When I arrived in Delhi on Wednesday afternoon, December 14, I commissioned a taxi to take me to Hotel Ranjit, the same hotel where I stayed overnight many years before. In twenty years how things had changed! The hotel was remodeled and unrecognizable were it not for its sign. And Delhi had come a long way toward Westernization. After a night's rest, I boarded the Rishikesh northbound bus at the Interstate Bus Terminal. Within a few hours, I was in Rishikesh experiencing the spiritual climate of my nostalgic reverie. It was not long before I found my way across the Lakshman Jhula Bridge, crossing the Ganges River; then walking about one kilometer past the Kailashanand Mission into the jungle foothills to the secluded retreat of the Tat Wale Baba Ashram.

There I met Swami Shankardasji, the beloved disciple who has spent most of his life in devoted service to his guru, and who remains in constant service as caretaker of the ashram. I introduced myself and explained how my visit with Tat Wale Baba years ago had made a profound impression on me. I asked the Swami if I could interview him since I was anxious to hear every detail of Tat Wale Baba's life. Swami Shankardasji complied. Since there were no other visitors present it was an opportune time for us to chat. Swami began by explaining that because of Tat Wale Baba's reclusive nature, and reluctance to talk about himself, little is known about his past. Swami Shankardasji shared the following information with me.

Kailashanand Mission towers above the tree line in the Himalayan foothills.
Photograph by Vincent J. Daczynski

Tat Wale Baba was born of spiritual parents who were middle class farmers in Punjab, India. The exact date of Tat Wale Baba's birth is not known. An estimate places his birth at about 1890. Tat Wale Baba received little formal education, spending most of his early childhood assisting his parents with farmwork. At about the age of eight or nine years, Tat Wale Baba's innate spiritual nature led him to begin meditating. This he did ardently whenever time permitted between chores. As he grew into his teenage years Tat Wale Baba took on a mesomorphic stature. Because of his physical prowess his friends encouraged him to join the Army, which he did. He did not like military life. Therefore, after just two months of military service he left the Army. Directly from the Army he sought the reclusive, sadhu lifestyle for himself. His search for a guru to guide him was fulfilled when he met Sri Jagannath Dasji at Ayodhya, the "Kingdom of Rama." This guru named

5

him Sri Mahavir Dash Ji. However, later, when Tat Wale Baba started wearing jute people called him Tat Wale, meaning "one who wears jute." The sobriquet stuck.

Swami Shankardasji greats me at the stairs leading to the Tat Wale Baba Ashram.
Photograph by Vincent J. Daczynski.

Tat Wale Baba lived at his guru's ashram for about three months during which time he was initiated into Raja Yoga. However, life at this ashram was too hectic for the serious meditation Tat Wale Baba sought. There were too many disciples and cows milling about, and the general noise of an active ashram caused too much disturbance for him. So, Tat Wale Baba left his guru's abode in search of a more reclusive retreat. After a few months' search he arrived at Rishikesh where his parents frequently attended Swargashram (a dense complex of cafes, shops and ashrams) for meditation. He thought this might be an ideal place for his meditations as well. However, as before, he found too many disturbances from the many visitors to this complex. After only a short stay he again sought a more reclusive refuge, and went to a remote ashram. There, he found the ambient peace he required. However, living at this site was harsh. Firewood was not easily available to provide warmth, and for cooking. Other essentials, such as food and water, were not readily available. The time and effort required to provide for himself disturbed his long periods of deep meditation.

Swami Shankardasji leaves his sandals at
the foot of the steps that lead to the Ashram.

Tat Wale Baba wearing jute. c. age twenty (1910).
Photograph provided by Swami Shankardasji. Photographer unknown.
Image used herein pursuant to "Fair Use" provision of
the United States Code 17, Section 107 Copyright Law.

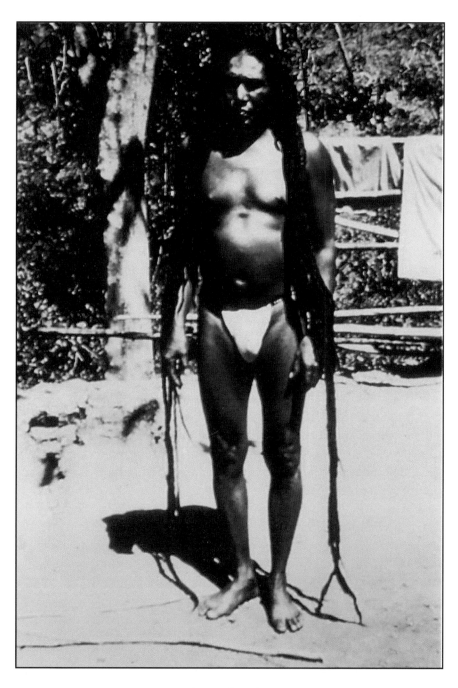

Tat Wale Baba
Photograph provided by Swami Shankardasji. Photographer unknown.
Image used herein pursuant to "Fair Use" provision of
the United States Code 17, Section 107 Copyright Law.

For days Tat Wale Baba sat near the Ganges River wondering where he would find a retreat that was fully suitable for his purpose. He was intuitively, or perhaps divinely, guided to Manikut Mountain. There he came upon an old, emaciated man with very long hair living in a cave. Tat Wale Baba approached the man and was invited to sit and talk. Their conversation lasted several hours. At the conclusion of their talk the old man left saying that his time was finished, and that he was going to the Himalayas to take mahasamadhi. He left the cave for Tat Wale Baba to occupy.

The cave was ideal for Tat Wale Baba. It had only a tiny opening which was barely visible from the passing trail. If the opening was sealed from within by a rock the cave was secluded completely. The cave was also conveniently located near a freshwater spring. And, its location of about two kilometers from Swargashram made it easy for Tat Wale Baba to go there to obtain his food supply. However, after some time, Tat Wale Baba felt that the daily trips to the ashram for food were too disturbing for him. So, he decided to forage for food in the ambient forest where he found kandamula leaves and roots, and fruits to sustain him. He foraged for food only occasionally, gathering a sufficient supply to last him for several days at a time. He ate sparingly during these secluded periods of long silence. Tat Wale Baba's regular schedule of meditating was from 2:00 a.m. until 10:00 a.m. From 10:00 a.m. until noon he would eat and rest. Then, from noon until 4:00 p.m. he would again meditate. He would exercise for about two hours, until 6:00 p.m. For exercise he usually took long walks of about ten kilometers, collected firewood, and worked hard at expanding the dimensions of his cave. He only did a few *asanas* (yoga postures). Instead, he preferred to meditate.

People who came into the forest to gather leaves and sticks for sale in Rishikesh occasionally spotted Tat Wale Baba emerging from his retreat. Word soon spread that a yogi was taking long periods of silence in a cave. As a result, pilgrims began to come by the hundreds to try to visit Tat Wale Baba. Because of the demand for his time, he changed his schedule to enable visitors to see him. He posted a sign stating that he would speak with visitors from 10:00 a.m. until noon, and then from 4:00 p.m. until 6:00 p.m. The rest of the time he remained in his cave, or did his chores and exercised.

Tat Wale Baba's cave is located a short stroll from this famous Parmarth Niketan Ashram.

Many life-size statues grace the Parmarth Niketan Ashram.
Above Photographs by Vincent J. Daczynski

CHAPTER 2

A Cobra for a Pet

Swami Shankardasji does dish washing chores at top of stairs,
outside of the entrance to the Tat Wale Baba Ashram.
Photograph by Vincent J. Daczynski.

I continued my interview with Swami Shankardasji, "I heard a rumor that Tat Wale Baba had a giant cobra snake for a pet. Was that true?"

"Yes. The snake was twice this long," Swami said as he extended his hands to the limit at each side of his body.

"That would make the snake about twelve feet long," I confirmed.

"Yes, and it was so big." To illustrate its girth Swami joined his finger tips of both hands, forming a circle about six inches in diameter.

"My guru would feed it milk. The snake would come and take milk from the cup. He liked to stay in the cave where my guru would meditate. But when my guru entered the cave, the snake would leave. He would come down through a crack and emerge at a hole which was here." Standing in the main room of the ashram, about twenty feet below Tat Wale Baba's cave, Swami pointed to where the exit hole was. "The snake would rest inside the crack with his head sticking out of the hole by about a foot. My guru had the hole sealed because people coming to see him were disturbed at the sight of the snake."

"Is the snake still here?"

A crystal-clear spring provides ample water
through a pipe to the Ashram.

"Yes," Swami continued. "There are two now. I think one is male and the other female. I hear the rustle of brush as they play above the ashram. Then they come down. They give me much trouble. Sometimes, when I open my eyes after meditating, I jump when I see a snake resting just a few inches from my feet. I never know where the snakes are. They come in and out of the ashram as they please. There are many cracks and openings by which they can enter."

"Do they ever take an attacking position?"

"No, they are friendly. But I stay away from them to avoid a mistake."

"Where are they now?"

"Sleeping for the winter. Once the weather warms, they come here often."

"There is a story circulating that Tat Wale Baba had contacted the King of the Cobras and asked him to make sure that no cobra would harm anyone. Is there any truth to that?" I asked.

"Yes, and I know of no snake bites to anyone in this area," Swami said confidently.

Steps inside of the Ashram lead to Tat Wale Baba's meditation cave.
Photograph by Vincent J. Daczynski.

CHAPTER 3

A Man of Miracles

Years earlier I heard a rumor that two Germans who visited Tat Wale Baba asked him about the hierarchy overseeing the universe. In answering the question Tat Wale Baba clapped his hands together and upon separating them widely, a vision of the celestial hierarchy appeared between his outstretched hands. Terrified by the means of reply, the two Germans ran away screaming down the mountain. Having heard this story second hand, I wanted confirmation. Swami Shankardasji replied, "Yes, he was capable of such miracles."

I asked, "Can you tell me of some of the other miracles that Tat Wale Baba performed?"

Swami stated, "I was sick, the sickest that I have ever been in my entire life. I thought I was to die. I had a severe headache. It felt like spikes were being driven at each side of my head," Swami explained as he pushed his closed fists, clutching invisible spikes, against his temples. "My head and body were like fire," he continued. "I was too sick to even take toilet," he said smiling, a little embarrassed by his own candor. "I soiled myself in bed. Then, around 4:00 a.m., I remember being startled by Tat Wale Baba appearing at my bed. And, somehow I found myself sitting at the edge of the bed before him."

"My guru put a cup to my forehead," Swami continued explaining as he showed with his right hand how the cup had been placed with its rim just between his eyebrows. "A white fluid came out of my head and filled the cup. My guru passed the cup to another person who was with him. I did not see the other person who was off to my left since my eyes were looking toward my guru. Again, my guru placed the cup at my head, just as before. White fluid came out, like milk. Again, he gave the cup to the person. Then again, he placed the cup at my head."

While speaking excitedly, as if the incident had occurred just the night before, Swami illustrated, by stretching out his hand, how Tat Wale Baba had passed the cup to his assistant. "Four times my guru did this," he said. "I felt like all my sins and karma had been taken away. My guru then stroked my forehead a few times with his hand. The next thing I knew I was looking at my guru's back as he was leaving the room. But my door was latched so that it could not open more than four inches. Yet, he passed easily through."

"How was he able to come in and go?" Swami asked rhetorically, testing my knowledge rather than showing his bewilderment – he very well knew about the *siddhis* (superhuman powers) that accomplished yogis possessed, whereby they may pass through walls at will.

Swami continued, "It was then that I realized that I was cured. To this day I have never been sick. I have not even had a headache." Swami Shankardasji paused, thinking awhile. "This incident happened around August or September in 1974, shortly before my guru took mahasamadhi."

Intrigued by the account, I asked Swami, "Are there any other miracles which Tat Wale Baba performed?"

"Yes," Swami answered. "There were three couples who could not bear children. Each couple came to see Tat Wale Baba, and from Guru's blessings each had a child born to them. One couple was from Punjab, the other from Delhi and the other from Haryana. This happened over a period of several years."

Another incident told by Swami Shankardasji also involved a healing miracle performed by Tat Wale Baba. "I think his name was Wilkins (author not using his real name)," Swami recalled. "He was Canadian. He was very sick, and saw many doctors. But none could help him. One day, just by chance, Wilkins had read in a book about Tat Wale Baba. And, in the book was a picture of Tat Wale Baba. Then, one day the Canadian got a dream of Tat Wale Baba wearing jute. Tat Wale Baba told him to take certain medication. The Canadian went and purchased the medication, and took it. After two days his stomach was clean. After one month the Canadian was completely healed. After that," Swami continued, "the Canadian went in search of Tat Wale Baba. Finally, he tracked him to this ashram, but Tat Wale Baba was dead. The Canadian stayed here for one month, meditating. One day while he meditated, he had a vision of Tat Wale Baba saying that he came too late. This happened in 1977 or 1978." Swami Shankardasji looked into the distance as he refreshed his memory, then confirmed, "It was 1977."

Following this story Swami Shankardasji offered me tea. I accepted graciously. By now the sun was beginning to set and an evening peacefulness blanketed the forest retreat. As I sipped my tea, I wondered why such a remarkable yogi would have met with the tragic death that he did.

Swami Shankardasji's puja to Tat Wale Baba
Background photo of Tat Wale Baba was taken four days prior to his murder.
Photograph of this puja was taken by Vincent J. Daczynski.

CHAPTER 4

A Tragic Death

On December 2, 1974 as he went to take his bath at 4:00 a.m., Sri Tat Wale Baba was murdered by a crazy gunman. I soon learned of the incident from my friend, Charlie Lutes. I wondered about the facts surrounding this crime, and why somebody would want to kill Tat Wale Baba. I heard various accounts, but none satisfied me. My visit with Swami Shankardasji afforded me the opportunity for an accurate account.

"What happened to Tat Wale Baba?" I probed a bit apprehensively as I felt I might be approaching a sensitive subject. But, Swami Shankardasji was open to my questioning.

"He was killed by a man living there in the mountains," Swami related as he gestured gently with his finger to give me an indication of the direction. Then, Swami shocked me when he said, "He still lives here, nearby."

My jaw dropped in shocked disbelief. I wondered if I had heard correctly. "How's that possible? Don't the police know he did it?"

"Oh yes! The police got him to confess. The man spent one year in prison, then paid "bail" and now is out."

I still had difficulty believing that a convicted murderer of a great yogi, in a spiritual country which cherishes its beacons of wisdom, could wiggle his way into freedom and be permitted to live on the same mountain where he executed his maleficent deed. "What a mockery!" I thought.

Swami continued, "This man had another run-in with the police. But, after a few months in prison, he again got out on parole." Swami Shankardasji brought out newspaper clippings that he had saved which reported the killing of Tat Wale Baba, and the subsequent crimes of this murderous renegade. "This last December 14, he again just got out of prison," Swami said. "It was his third time. And he is still causing problems for people here."

I now could understand why Swami Shankardasji made it a practice to bolt the ashram door shut. It was hard to imagine that one needed to protect oneself against the harm from others while on a spiritual retreat in a cave hidden in the Himalayan jungles overlooking a holy city. The cobras, however, are friendly! Be that as it may.

Swami Shankardasji, following the example of his guru who never spoke ill of anyone, asked me not to describe Tat Wale Baba's murderer or to mention the other crimes of which this killer had been convicted. He only wanted me to present the minimum facts necessary to explain, simply, the death of his guru. This was a very noble gesture, indeed, considering the severity of the incident and the opportunity through my writings for him to tell all

Swami Shankardasji stands at monument where Tat Wale Baba was murdered. Photograph was provided by Swami Shankardasji. Photographer unknown. Image used herein pursuant to "Fair Use" provision of the United States Code 17, Section 107 Copyright Law.

"Why did he do it?" I asked, continuing my inquiry

"The man was crazy with jealousy. He tried to set himself up as a great saint and wanted people to go to his ashram. But few went to see him. He noticed people from all over the world coming here to visit my guru. He thought that if he would kill my guru then people would go to see him instead."

Pausing to reflect awhile, Swami Shankardasji then said, "Twice my guru told me that he would be shot to death. But I did not give it a second thought. Maybe my mind could not accept what I was being told. But, after my guru was shot, I clearly remembered his words to me. He said that a rogue, who was very jealous of him, and living nearby in the forest, would sneak up and shoot him in the back. My guru told me this on June 22, 1971, several years before he took samadhi. Also, just two days before he was shot, my guru reminded me of this prediction. There were two other disciples present at this time."

CHAPTER 5

Sweet Memories

The sun had set and were it not for the electric torches provided by Swami, I would not be able to see my hand before my face. In keeping with the traditional Indian custom, Swami invited me to stay overnight. I readily accepted. Soon the night's darkness was accompanied by a chilling breeze which blew through the cracks in the cottage, causing whirlpools of leaves to stir on the concrete floor. About 8:00 p.m. Swami Shankardasji fixed me a bedroll of blankets and I snuggled in for the night. Not used to retiring so early, I lay awake recalling the time twenty years earlier when I had met Tat Wale Baba.

It was March 30, 1969. I was at Maharishi Mahesh Yogi's ashram, attending a course to become a teacher of the Transcendental Meditation Program. The ashram was located on a hill overlooking the Ganges, and about a couple of kilometers below Tat Wale Baba's ashram. There were 120 other people from all parts of the world also attending Maharishi's training course. News quickly spread that Maharishi Mahesh Yogi had invited "the wise man of the mountains," Tat Wale Baba, to come visit us that afternoon. In the early afternoon we all anxiously waited for our guest to arrive.

At the appointed time several ochre-robed men made their way toward the lecture hall. Along with them was Maharishi Mahesh Yogi who was accompanied by Tat Wale Baba, a muscular golden brown skinned Adonis. Also joining along were some of the course participants. Tat Wale Baba's features were much like that of an American Indian. He was naked except for an ochre loincloth which was held around his waist with a brass chain. His black braided hair flowed down his back and was so long that, were it not carried by an attendant, it would have trailed along the ground. The unworldly beauty of this man was unsurpassed by any individual that I had ever seen. I can best compare him with the godlike men depicted in mythology. Tat Wale Baba was also called Mahavir Dash, meaning "Hanuman, servant of Rama."

He appeared no older than in his thirties, yet he was said to be about eighty years old. He exuded a radiant aura as he took a majestic cross-legged position on a small platform which was covered with a deerskin. Maharishi and the others took their seats and we all waited anxiously to hear rishi Sri Tat Wale Baba speak. For a while Tat Wale Baba sat with a downcast gaze, almost indifferent to our presence. I had just stood up and was walking through the audience to gain a better camera angle when Tat Wale Baba resounded with a long drawn out AAAaauuuummmmm. I froze in the middle of taking a stride as the reverberation consumed me. I was motionless and breathless, momentarily suspended in deep transcendental silence.

Tat Wale Baba delivers discourse to Maharishi Mahesh Yogi's students
at Maharishi's Academy of Meditation, Rishikesh, 1969.
Maharishi Mahesh Yogi translates.
Photograph by Vincent J. Daczynski.

It was only after the conclusion of the intonation that I was aroused from my entrancement, and completed my stride. However, I was too awestruck by the experience to take more pictures, and just sat down to hear what this great Rishi had to say.

Tat Wale Baba began his discourse in unstrained, forceful Hindi, and Maharishi Mahesh Yogi translated.

What is the aim of all the beings? It is the attainment of infinite happiness. A life free from suffering and the attainment of eternal happiness is what we want. Now, we should discriminate and analyze if there is anything in the world which can give us permanent, eternal happiness. From the ant up to the giant of the Creator, all are in the field of change, that is, relative values. Infinite happiness can only come from something which could be immortal, nonchanging, eternal. This which is the goal of everything, this infinite, is our own *Self*. And in order to experience that *Self* which

22

is the basis of all, we don't have to seek, we don't have to search, we don't have to make efforts. It's there, present everywhere. Wherever you are, in whatever reign of time or place, that *Self* is there – wherever we are in whatever time. Only, we have to take our awareness to that level and that is it. Having forgotten that level of life, we are seeking for that eternal happiness. That *Self* is. It is *being* and it is blissful. Having forgotten that, we now are seeking for it. We have forgotten what we ourselves are and we're trying to find that in the world. As long as we don't enter into that area which is infinite happiness, free from suffering, so long we will not be free from suffering and we will not get into that eternal happiness. There is no happiness of significant nature in the world; the child is gone, and the youth is gone, and the man is old, and even then, he is not fulfilled in the world. When he gets established in the *Self*, then automatically freedom from suffering and attainment of bliss will be there.

Tat Wale Baba continues with his discourse to Maharishi Mahesh Yogi's students.
Photograph by Vincent J. Daczynski.

Maharishi Mahesh Yogi interjected, "The thing is very important which he says now!"

That which is omnipresent doesn't have to be sought. It's there already. Start to *be*. That which is omnipresent is not to be sought; only our awareness has to be brought to that level and that bliss is there. You don't have to seek it. Understand? Unless we get into that omnipresent bliss, satisfaction is not going to come. If it were to come, it would have come by now through so many avenues in the world.

But, it has not. Therefore, that which is the *Self* is your own *being*. You don't have to look in the outside. And, it is irrespective of any religious faiths or beliefs; Christians or Mormons or Hindus. That *being* is the knowledge itself. Only, you have to know.

All these various manifestations of happiness that we experience in the world, they also are the manifestations of the same eternal *being* which is our own *Self*. If we are aware of the *Self*, if we know it, fine. Otherwise, we have to *be*. And, therefore, it is necessary to bring our awareness deep within ourselves. As deeply as we can bring our awareness to the *Self*, so intensely we can inherit that which is omnipresent in our day-to-day life. Having known that *Self* we will be eternally contented; remaining in the world we will live contentment. And, it's not a matter of detaching ourselves from the world. Only, we have to know *It*, and having known *It*, then, all different manifestations in the world will be experienced as manifestations of *That*. We don't have to detach ourselves. It is just a matter of bringing the awareness to that area, and *be*, and live *It*.

Having gained this beautiful, perfect human nervous system, if we have known that element of the *Self*, then we have really used this wonderful diamond-like gift, this diamond-like nervous system which is capable of giving that eternal bliss. If it is not experienced, then we have wasted that gift of diamond. We have taken upon ourselves this human nervous system, not for the sake of petty enjoyment of changing nature in this relative field of change, but to live and be that infinite bliss. And, we will have to attain that thing whether we attain it in this life, or in the next, or in the next. We just can't forego that. Therefore, with the assistance of the guru and the scriptures, better to attain it quickly. Why postpone?

Tat Wale Baba's talk was followed by an opportunity for questions to be asked.

CHAPTER 6

Simple Truths

Tat Wale Baba answers students' questions.
Photograph by Vincent J. Daczynski.

As each question was asked in English Maharishi Mahesh Yogi translated to Hindi, then translated Tat Wale Baba's replies.

Student: Can he tell us of his master and the tradition he follows?

TWB: The *Self* is free from any tradition or non-tradition.

MMY (adding his own comment): He is from the tradition of Shukadev. Shukadev was like him, not of this world. Away from it.

Student: Can he tell us what kind of meditation he does?

TWB: I am established in Vedanta and that way we talk about it, and we *be*. There is no practice as such.

Student: What do you think about Transcendental Meditation?

TWB: Transcendental Consciousness is the basis of all experience. Pure Consciousness is *That* through which we experience. *That* is not a thing which one can experience. And, all this world is in a state of Pure Consciousness, and it is through *That* that we experience everything. Pure Consciousness, or Transcendental Consciousness, is nothing that we experience. Through *That* we are experiencing everything. *That* is the basis of all experience, and experiencing; so, enjoy that state.

Student: Is it possible to increase one's capacity to enjoy that state?

TWB: We can increase it to any great extent through meditation. And as we go deeper, *That* will shine forth in our life outside. So, it's possible to increase our ability to be *That*. And, that is through meditation.

Student: Does he have any techniques that he teaches his disciples?

TWB: We are sitting in the forest, and when we are sitting in the forest, we have some purpose to perform, and with that we are sitting. If some seeker comes and asks, fine. We give advice. Otherwise, we don't have much time. We are in the forest, and we are in the forest for some purpose. But, if some seeker comes, fine. His doubts are cleared and removed.

Student: Does he think that his way of life helps the rest of mankind or only him?

TWB: All these saints meditating and established in the *Self*, they are the basis for all this running of the entire universe, and they are the basis of the whole thing; and not for themselves alone. Their good vibrations are influencing societies for their advancement.

Student: Like a powerhouse?

TWB: Like a powerhouse. The powerhouse is in Delhi and the bulb is shining here. It is not the bulb that is shining. It's the power from the powerhouse. It is the saints established in their *Self* who are infusing life into the whole universe. And, it is they who have found *Smriti Purananam* (Vedic codes of behavior). It is they who have found the essentials, the realities of life, and have taught to the world various conducts of living; ways of realization of the *Self*, ways of realization of God, and all these higher states of life. It is they who have brought wisdom home to the world, and they are at the basis of all the increasing prosperity of the world through their vibrations and through their attainment.

Student: How much sleep does he require?

TWB: If *I* sleep what will happen to the world? Asleep and awake: the sleep and awake is the nature of the mind. Sometimes the mind sleeps, sometimes it is awake. If *I* sleep, the whole basis of the world would be sleeping and then there will be left nothing. So, *I* don't sleep. If someone sleeps it is the mind. The *Self* doesn't sleep. All these states of waking, dreaming; they belong to the mind. They are not the state of the *Self*. And, if you speak of my sleeping, *I* don't sleep because the *Self* doesn't sleep. If the *Self* sleeps, then the whole world would go into sleep.

Student: Is there any difference between the time that he is meditating and the time when he is not meditating, in how he feels, or his interaction with the environment?

TWB: Meditating for some time, one gets established permanently in the state of *being*. And then, wherever the mind goes one is established in that *Self* no matter what one does here or there; it doesn't matter when one is established in the *Self*. And, that state comes after some time from going deep inside and coming out. With this practice one gets established permanently in the *Self;* and then whatever you do you are not separate from the *Self*.

Students: Are you living in that state now?

TWB: That which is unborn, eternal, we can't talk about it in terms of time. In terms of time the *Self* can't be talked.

Student: Does he feel that there is more to attain?

TWB: What is there to be gained or attained? That which is to be gained is omnipresent, and we are *That*, and it's already attained. As long as the mind has been wavering only in the changing relative, so long it was out of sight. And, when the mind has been concentrated and has attained to that level, nothing new has happened. The thing that was there, it is there. Nothing new has happened or has been attained. Nothing! That which was there is there even now, and was even before. Only the difference is in the mind; the mind was unaware of *That* and now the mind is aware. So, what is there to talk about attainment of further states?

Student: Can he tell us of the love that flows from one's heart once the state is attained?

TWB: One's love overflows. As one loves himself so does he begin to love others. Because in that state there is none other than one's *Self*. Therefore, one's love for one's *Self* is one's love for others. And then, whatever communications are there, they are communications in one's own *Self*.

The *Self* is golden. It is only a matter of taking our awareness to *That* and then the criterion for *That* will be that we will begin to display all love and harmony in the field of all our action and experience. That will be the criterion. When the love increases, that becomes the balance to measure that we are nearing *That*. Otherwise, the thing is already there, only we have to incorporate it in our lives. We have to exhibit more of love, more of happiness. Expression of *That* is necessary, otherwise the state of *That* is already there. And, we will begin to express more of *It* when we become more aware of *It*.

Student: Can we meditate with you?

Tat Wale Baba closed his eyes and we all meditated for about twenty minutes. Then, the opportunity to ask more questions resumed.

Student: What do you see for the future of the world?

TWB: We have to create future. Future does not have to create us. And, if we do good things and meditate and experience that *Self* and be omnipresent, future is going to be good. If we do not, we are going to create a bad future. We have to create the future. The future is in our hands.

Student: Will there be world peace?

The world is within you. And, if you are at peace within, if your awareness is established in your *Self* your world is in peace. And, if you are wavering and peaceless and you are not in tune with your own eternal state of *Being* then the world is in peacelessness. If you want to create peace on the cosmic level then you must take refuge in God. And, if you want peace within yourself, realize the *Self* and your world will be in peace and you will see that the whole world is in peace. The world is as you are, and the world will be as you will be.

Student: Did a tiger ever bother you?

TWB: The tiger is the killer of the killer. If you have the tendency of violence then that tendency of the violence will itself become a tiger and will pounce upon you and kill you. And if you are established in that non-violence of the eternal being bliss consciousness of the *Self,* then no tiger will ever pounce upon you. It is our own karma that acts as the tiger that pounces upon us, whether for good or for bad.

Student: Are there any shortcuts to purification of karma?

TWB: The shortest cut to the purification of karma is surrender to God, devotion to God, realization of the *Self*. And, when you realize the *Self* all your mind and senses will be purified. And, when your senses are purified all your actions will be good. They will be life supporting. They behave with you as your friends. And, if the mind is not established in the *Self*, in the glory of God, then your own senses

28

will become your enemy. And then, all your karma will pounce upon you as your enemy. It is the fixity of the mind in the *Self* that makes your senses your friend, and non-fixity of the mind in the *Self* makes your senses your enemy. Senses-enemy means karma, because the karma is performed by the senses. So, the karma will be good if the mind is established in the *Self* and karma will not be good if the mind is not established in the *Self*.

Practice. Increase your practice to arrive at that goal.

Student: Is it a liability to be a householder and do this practice?

TWB: Householder's way of life is not bad. But, not being able to live up to the standards of this lifestyle we make a hell out of ourselves in a householder's way of life.

Student: Is it possible to work in the world when we have gained the highest state of pure supreme knowledge?

TWB: There are two ways of life, householder and recluse. Those who are in the householder's way of life, they by habit are engaged in activity, even having gained that state of supreme knowledge. And, those who are recluse by nature, they don't have anything to do with the activity of life. So, they continue to live that way. But, both live that state of supreme knowledge.

Student: Is it possible that one who lives a householder's way of life can then desire to switch and live the life of a recluse? Or, would this cause a conflict?

TWB: The ideal condition would be not to enter into the household. If you want to become a *sannyasi* (renunciate), or, if you have entered the householder's life, then share the responsibility that you have taken with the wife and children, and then complete that responsibility. Get your children educated and be done with the whole thing. Then, it would be good to waver off from there. Otherwise, don't enter it, and that will be the more ideal. Having taken the responsibility it won't be good to shut that responsibility.

Tat Wale Baba exits the lecture hall after delivering his discourse.
Photograph by Vincent J. Daczynski.

Tat Wale Baba heads back to his ashram cave.
Photograph by Vincent J. Daczynski.

As I lay tucked warmly inside my bedroll, reviewing my memories, it was hard to believe that twenty years had passed since I had heard these simple truths spoken by Tat Wale Baba. After about two hours of nostalgic dreaming I drifted into a deep sleep.

CHAPTER 7

And then There Was One

The sepulcher of Tat Wale Baba
Photograph by Vincent J. Daczynski.

I was startled from my sleep early the following morning by the ruckus play of two small nocturnal creatures that found their way into the ashram cabin. It was still too dark to see. But, being wide-awake, I decided to make my way to the tomb of Tat Wale Baba. I crawled slowly along the floor toward the opening of the adjacent cave where the tomb was located. As I entered the cave, I felt an awesome mystical power emanating from Tat Wale Baba's tomb. The power was so intense it was like the force of energy one would experience when approaching a furnace. I positioned myself in the cave, taking a seated posture, in front of the tomb. With the mystical energy infusing intensely into me, I meditated absorbing its influence. I quickly fell into a deep, very deep, state of meditation. My back remained straight, although unsupported. I sat motionless, as if frozen into a statuelike position by this unseen force. Five hours passed as if only a half-hour. I was aware of the onset of dawn and of Swami Shankardasji arising and taking care of his morning chores and meditation. Yet, I remained deeply entranced, overwhelmed by the profound inner peace of the meditation experience.

At about 8:00 a.m. I emerged from my meditation just when Swami Shankardasji was beginning his practice of asanas in the adjoining room. I watched Swami do his routine. He was an adept. His balance was perfect as he gracefully moved from one complex posture to another. As I watched I admired Swami Shankardasji for his style of life. As a youth I had considered living a reclusive life as a yogi in a mountain retreat, away from the fast-paced rat race world of material pursuits. Here was a man living the yogi life, dedicated to spiritual unfoldment. I watched his every move, vicariously experiencing his life.

His life was very simple. There was no electricity or gas to supply artificial heat or light. Firewood lit in a small fireplace provided fire for cooking. Toilet was taken in the forest. A nearby perpetual waterfall provided a daily refreshing shower. A pipe leading from this cascade captured a sufficient flow and pressure of water to provide a steady flowing fountain at the ashram gate. Swami's diet was as simple as his lifestyle. Sometimes he would eat the leaves, roots and fruits provided by the ambient forest. Mostly, he prepared simple vegetarian meals of vegetables and grains. He ate sparingly, taking one or two light meals daily. Yet, he had a strong, muscular build.

His life was unencumbered with such worldly essentials as automobiles, televisions, laptops and the wide array of consumer products the Western world just cannot do without. Swami was content with the little he had. He lived his life just as Tat Wale Baba did. Although short on material comforts, he was filled with compassion and love as he cared for his departed guru's ashram. After Swami Shankardasji finished his morning routine there was time and opportunity for us to talk some more. I resumed the line of questioning that I had followed the day before.

"How old was Tat Wale Baba? Was he really as old as he's said to have been?"

"It is difficult to say," replied Swami, "because no known records exist and Tat Wale Baba stopped aging after he reached around thirty-five years of age." Swami continued, "A man who was a classmate of Tat Wale Baba's in elementary school, and who had seen Tat Wale Baba later in life, commented that Tat Wale Baba had stopped aging. The man died recently and he was about ninety-five years old."

By assuming that Tat Wale Baba was of equal age as this classmate I estimated Tat Wale Baba's year of birth to have been about 1890. "That would place Tat Wale Baba's age at about eighty-five years when he was killed," I stated, looking for a confirmation from Swami.

"That is about right," he said.

"How did you meet Tat Wale Baba?"

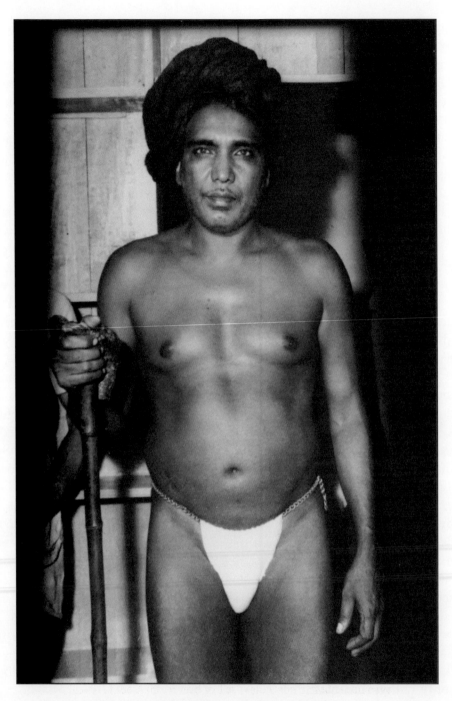

Tat Wale Baba. c. age forty (1930).
Photograph provided by Swami Shankardasji. Photographer unknown.
Image used herein pursuant to "Fair Use" provision of
the United States Code 17, Section 107 Copyright Law.

Swami gleamed as he recalled this precious moment in his life. "I was seven years old when I left home in search of Lord Shiva. I wandered all over India and, finally, some yogi told me to do tapasya in the Himalayan Mountains; then, maybe I would find God. So, in 1965 I went to Rishikesh and stayed at Swargashram. There, I read in a book that without a guru it is not possible to get *moksha* (liberation) and Brahman realization. My search for my guru intensified. I went to the Manikut Mountain to do tapasya, still hoping to find Lord Shiva. As I came up the mountain, I saw Tat Wale Baba sitting on a stone in the front of his cave. He looked to me like Lord Shiva. When I saw him my heart and body started to shake, and I became very afraid. I ran away into the forest and took refuge under a tree, until evening, when I returned to Swargashram. For the next three days I sat near the Ganga. I read the Gita and fasted, drinking only Ganga water. I prayed to God for guidance. I returned to Tat Wale Baba's cave. I was no more afraid. We looked at each other simultaneously. He smiled at me, and I immediately felt close to him. So, I stayed, and I have been with him since."

Swami got up and reached into a folder from which he withdrew an album of pictures. He showed me his collection of photos. "I'm putting together a book of pictures so visitors can see a history of Tat Wale Baba's life."

From that statement one idea led to another and the impetus for writing this book was born. Swami Shankardasji and I chatted for several more hours. "I don't usually talk so much," he said.

However, with my time quickly slipping away I needed to press for more information. "Did Tat Wale Baba do asanas?" I asked.

"Not usually. He preferred long meditations to asanas," replied Swami.

"Did he teach any techniques?"

"Yes," Swami said. "After I was in Tat Wale Baba's service for two months, he gave me initiation and taught me some meditation techniques. He taught different techniques for sadhus, different techniques for yogis and different techniques for the general people. He also gave out general knowledge. For example, when a visitor once asked him how to control the mind, he said that you can't stop desire because it is like trying to stop the Ganges. He said to let the mind flow. But wherever the mind goes there also see your God, your personal God. That way your mind automatically comes back to the concentration on the goal, God.

"Tat Wale Baba said when you work do everything in the name of God, everything for God," continued Swami. "Never help anyone for the fruits, only as service to God. Then, that which is good for you, God will give himself. In this way people will become as children of a cat: whatever a kitten needs, the mother cat immediately provides. Otherwise, they will be like a baby monkey where the mother is running and jumping and the baby must wait or chase after it for nurturing."

Swami then added, "Tat Wale Baba advised people to put their attention on their guru or God – such as Jesus, Rama, Krishna – while they perform action. By doing so they will gain the ideal of God or guru in their actions."

"Did Tat Wale Baba have any disciples?"

Swami replied, "He only had eleven disciples at the time of his death. But he has thousands of devotees in India as well as in many foreign countries throughout the world. Each year, on December 2, the day when my guru took samadhi, hundreds of people come here in remembrance of him."

Although hundreds of people come annually and thousands around the world love him, only Swami Shankardasji remains as the sole caretaker of the Tat Wale Baba ashram. Hidden in the secluded jungle cover of the Himalayan foothills he remains devoted and in continued service maintaining the tradition of his guru.

Swami Shankardasji maintains a daily puja to his Guru Dev.
Photograph by Vincent J. Daczynski.

CHAPTER 8

His Light Still Shines

"We have not eaten in over twenty-four hours," Swami Shankardasji realized as our conversation continued into the afternoon. "Let's take our meal now," he suggested, "We can continue talking later."

I concurred and Swami went into the adjacent room to prepare supper for us. He returned after a while with a mound of *aloo gobi* (cauliflower and potatoes with spices) on a large platter. He handed me the platter and stood nearby waiting for me to eat.

Noticing that he had no platter for himself I asked, "Aren't you eating?"

"Yes," he said, "but first I want to make sure you are satisfied with your meal. Is it spiced okay for you? Would you care for some more salt?"

"No. This is fine," I said, still perplexed at why he had no food for himself.

After Swami was assured that I was satisfied with his culinary skills he left the room to eat alone in the kitchen. It was then that I realized that Swami Shankardasji preferred to eat alone. I thought about this and wondered how many digestive and gastrointestinal disorders might be solved or prevented if everyone ate alone – no arguing or bickering while eating, or gulping of food to get one's word into a brisk conversation. I concluded that silence during mealtime has to have a positive influence on health.

After about a half-hour Swami Shankardasji returned, offering me seconds. But I was satisfied, and more concerned with shifting back to our conversation which resumed after a brief time of clean up.

"Tell me something more about Tat Wale Baba," I asked, hoping that my broad question would bring new information to light.

Swami Shankardasji thought for a while, then replied, "Tat Wale Baba's desire was to bring humanity and all religions together for peace in the world. He foresaw this site as the future center of the world, and where he would direct the people, bringing new message for the benefit of the world. Unfortunately, his work was unfinished here when he suddenly left. He was in the process of building more caves for meditation."

After a long reflective pause Swami continued, "This place is very special. According to the Shiva Puranas it was in this area that Lord Shiva stopped for rest with his party of gods and sages while on his way to marry Sati in Haridwar. There is speculation among some swamis that the cave which was used by Tat Wale Baba was the *Bhut Nath Gufa* (cave of Shiva)."

I noticed a spiritual power emanating, not only from the tomb of Tat Wale Baba, but also from the ashram. Perhaps this emanation lends credence to the ancient mythology of the Shiva Puranas and the folklore passed down through generations of swamis.

Tat Wale Baba sayings are prominently displayed at the entrance to the Ashram.
Photograph by Vincent J. Daczynski.

Swami Shankardasji explained, "Some people who come here go crazy. They say they can't stay, and run out."

I responded with my theory, "I think it's the power, the high vibrations here. This causes them to feel very uncomfortable, so they want to run away."

"Maybe so," Swami acknowledged.

It was getting late and I needed to get some pictures before the onset of twilight. Swami Shankardasji took me outside and introduced me to one of his feathered friends, a *mayur* (peacock) with its splendid iridescent blue and green plumage. He fed it a piece of bread as I captured photos of this tender interaction between Swami and this usually very shy bird.

Then, Swami Shankardasji took me for a tour of the ashram grounds and showed me a series of eroded caves, which he planned to expand, that were hidden by the forest underbrush. In one of the smaller caves was a Shiva Lingam marking the site of the Sri Tat Wale Baba Ashram as Bhut Nath Gufa.

A mayur also enjoys the warm hospitality of Swami Shankardasji
Photograph by Vincent J. Daczynski.

Lesser caves below the ashram.
Photograph by Vincent J. Daczynski.

A Shiva Lingam marks the site of the Sri Tat Wale Baba Ashram as Bhut Nath Gufa.
Photograph by Vincent J. Daczynski.

"Hundreds of people come here every year," explained Swami Shankardasji as he continued the tour. "They come from all over India on December 2, in remembrance of Tat Wale Baba. Some foreigners also come."

We made our way to the flat concrete roof of the ashram cabin and watched as the sun nestled softly behind the Himalayan foothills.

Swami Shankardasji (center) with some of the many
devotees, who come annually to pay their respects to
Tat Wale Baba on December 2, the day of his mahasamadhi.
Photo provided by Swami Shankardasji. Photographer unknown.
Image used herein pursuant to "Fair Use" provision of
the United States Code 17, Section 107 Copyright Law.

Swami Shankardasji invited me to stay longer, but it was getting late. I still had to get back across the Ganges to my hotel to make preparations for my early morning bus departure to Delhi. I thanked Swami for his time and hospitality.

My visit to the Tat Wale Baba ashram was a very personal emotionally moving experience. My encounter with Tat Wale Baba many years earlier sparked a love in my heart for him that to this day has not dwindled.

Twilight view overlooking the Ganges from the patio of the Ashram
Photograph by Vincent J. Daczynski.

"Sometime when you have more time, when you come back, I will tell you more. There are many stories I can tell you," Swami said. "Also, by then, I should have a cave ready which you may use."

As I was leaving, my heart flowed to Swami Shankardasji. I felt as if I had gained a good friend. I pressed my palms together, fingers pointing upward, in front of my chest in the traditional Indian style. He returned the gesture. Then, smiling, in a show of affection, he extended his hand and gave me a hearty Western handshake.

I left with my heart fulfilled. For many years I had desired to visit the Tat Wale Baba Ashram and meditate there. My desire was finally realized. I also left reluctantly, already yearning for the next time when I could visit the Ashram to experience again the essence of Tat Wale Baba, the Himalayan great Rishi, whose spirit still radiates a guiding light for all who come seeking God.

On my journey back home, I thought of those days when I had met Sri Tat Wale Baba, and the time I spent in training with His Holiness Maharishi Mahesh Yogi to become a teacher of Transcendental Meditation to help bring the heretofore secret teaching of the Vedas to the Western world. Fortunately, today the knowledge of the Vedas no longer needs to be sought only in the context of a reclusive life in the Himalayas. The knowledge is now also readily available for all people throughout the world. What a great blessing for the world!

Author headed back home after a memorable overnight stay at the Tat Wale Baba Ashram.
Photograph by Vincent J. Daczynski.

To contact Swami Shankardasji:

Swami Shankardasji
Sri Tat Wale Baba Ashram
Bhut Nath Gufa
Post Swargashram
Rishikesh 249304, Upprakand
India

CHAPTER 9

Other Photos of Tat Wale Baba

Tat Wale Baba with Maharishi Mahesh Yogi
and Swami Satchidananda (115 years.old).
Image by Charles F. Lutes, April 13, 1968.

Image source unknown.
Tat Wale Baba (c.) Maharishi Mahesh Yogi (r.) and Brahmachari Devendra (l.).
Image used herein pursuant to "Fair Use" provision of
the United States Code 17, Section 107 Copyright Law.

Image source unknown.
Image used herein pursuant to "Fair Use" provision of
the United States Code 17, Section 107 Copyright Law.

Image source unknown.
Image used herein pursuant to "Fair Use" provision of
the United States Code 17, Section 107 Copyright Law.

Image source unknown.
Image used herein pursuant to "Fair Use" provision of
the United States Code 17, Section 107 Copyright Law.

Image source unknown.
Image used herein pursuant to "Fair Use" provision of
the United States Code 17, Section 107 Copyright Law.

Last known photo of Tat Wale Baba (estimated. age 85 years).
Photograph provided by Swami Shankardasji. Photographer unknown.

Above two images: source unknown.
Images used herein pursuant to "Fair Use" provision of
the United States Code 17, Section 107 Copyright Law.

Image source unknown.
Image used herein pursuant to "Fair Use" provision of
the United States Code 17, Section 107 Copyright Law.

Printed in Great Britain
by Amazon

20955071R10031